Wheels

Lada Kratky

ESL W2

Illustrated with photographs

HAMPTON-BROWN BOOKS

MANY CULTURES, MANY LANGUAGES…MANY POSSIBILITIES!™

Tricycle wheels
go around and around.

Bike wheels
go all around, too.

Car wheels
go around and around.

Truck wheels
go all around, too.

Train wheels
go around and around.

Plane wheels go
all around, too.

Skate wheels
go around and around.
Now I can go
all around, too!